DARLING BY STARLIGHT
RED EDITION
A poetry Collection by S.R. Butler

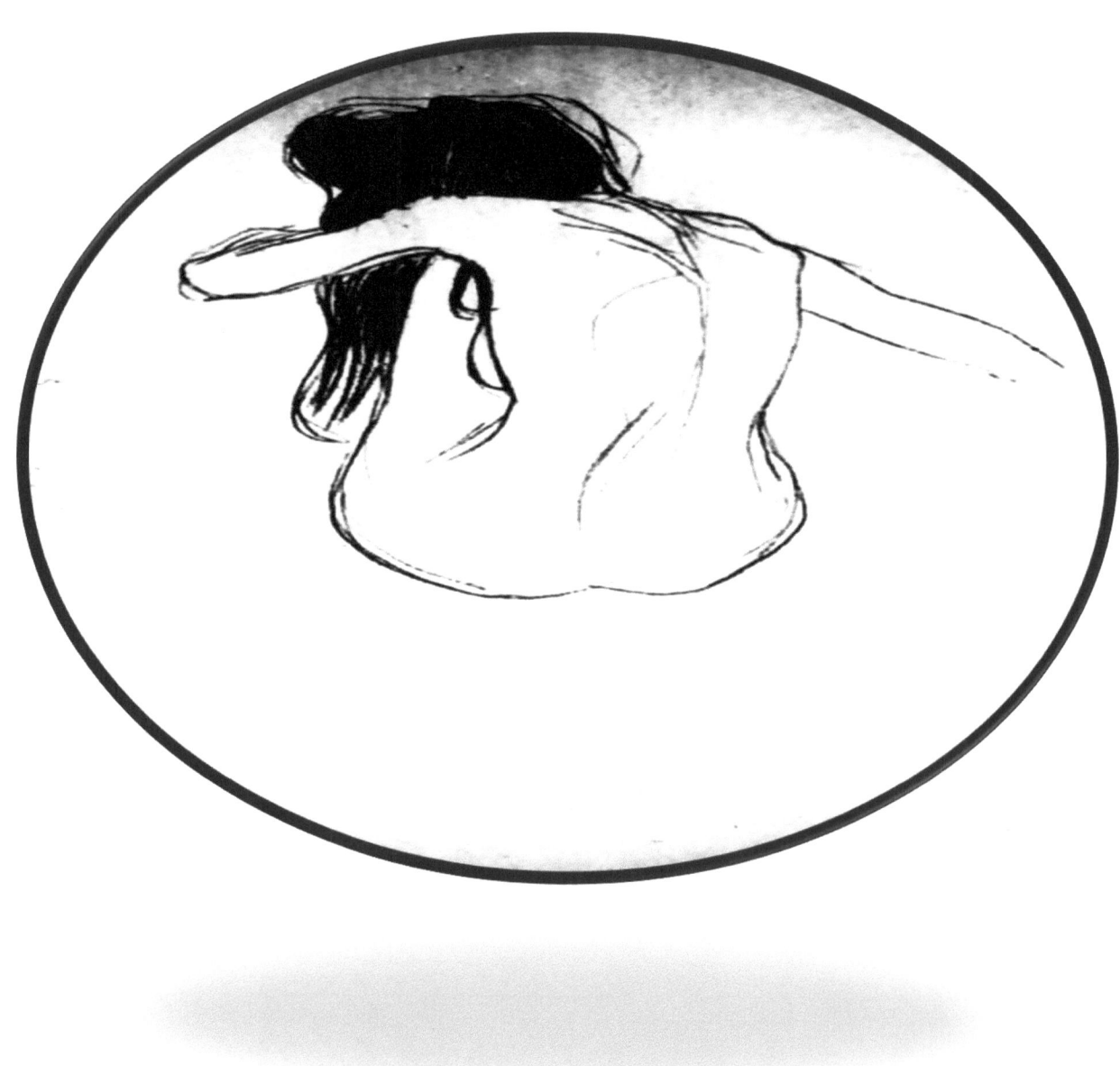

TICHBORNE PUBLISHING WORKS
West Palm Beach, Florida
ourmoviemade@gmail.com

All rights reserved. This book or any portion thereof may not be reproduced or used in any manner whatsoever without the express written permission of the publisher except for the use of brief quotations in a book review.

Printed in the United States of America - First Printing, 2016
ISBN-13: 978-0692665633 (Tichborne Publishing Works)
ISBN-10: 0692665633
Copyright © 2016 by S. R. Butler

Dedication

This to the only June that Johnny sees
This to the Monic like music and madness in their middle
The melody in their song

This to Marilyn and Jo
To the bleeding that proceeded
And the flowers that followed

This to it never was going to be easy
If it was never going to end

This to his Ophelia who opened our eyes before flooding lungs
This to every Delilah who held our hair

This to all messy surrender
Constanze covering Mozart in death
In hope for her own

This to the brutal thing worth dying for
Because the living is no better without it

This to Summer
And Venus
And all Goddesses, seasons or frauds before or after that

This to Cleopatra
This to Hatshepsut
Nefertiti
And every Bathsheba worth killing any everyman for

This to all women we can make more of

This to Will and Jada
And Tupac and Jada to lay the groundwork for that

To the Alma's who helped Hitchcock get the art right

Blondes may be more fun
But certainly are not more consistent

We would not be the same without you

To any Zelda that ever pushed a Fitzgerald to and past
Safe, success and sanity

Who grayed our hair
Who drove us drunk and competing to the grave

This to Silly Mrs. Rabbit that played Patty cake elsewhere
Only to return in time to bring Roger his happy end
And to turn his tragedy to comedy

To every and ONLY her
Who gave us the gift and fever of writing
A path toward immortality

This to my own Ilsa
And her Paris
And the distance that threatens
That I face with no damn "Good" byes
Because I will be there soon even if it is a lie

This because it only works when it is near impossible

This to my Josephine
This from Napoleon

This to prove the only power that cannot be rescinded
Is the power
I wield greater than any man you would or have allowed
This power
As evidenced in last words
My poetry, My War, My love, My Darling

See this?
It is for ALL of you

IN ORDER OF SERVICE

1. **DARLING BY STARLIGHT** 9
2. **1:27 AM (Till)** 11
3. **GENESIS (First Light)** 13
4. **11:13 PM** 15
5. **WHAT ESCAPES ME** 16
6. **PLEASURE DELAYER** 18
7. **10 PM EXACT (ABOUT KISSING)** 21
8. **WHERE IT CAME TO REST** 23
9. **"YES" TO EMPRESS SUBMISSION** 24
10. **WHERE THE FOX WILL HIDE** 27
11. **BLOODLUST GOODBYE** 29
12. **2:20 AM (Me On The Menu)** 31
13. **4:00AM (To The Lamb Named Her)** 33
14. **RED** 34
15. **11:58** 35
16. **GIVE ME YOUR SIN** 37
17. **KISS AT THE RIGHT TIME** 42
18. **2:43 AM** 43
19. **SOUTH HEAVEN / NORTH OF EDEN** 45
20. **3:46 AM (Planet me)** 47
21. **DEATH AS PROGRESS... A LOVE POEM** 49
22. *LAZY HORNS* 50
23. **DOUBLE NEGATIVE** 52
24. **I WILL LET HIM LIVE** 54
25. **OUR THERE?** 57
26. **MOLOCH** 58
27. **OEDIPUS BY HARP** 60
28. **IN PAST TENSE** 61
29. **WITH COLOR** 63
30. **3:11 AM (And Now I am Just Rambling)** 64
31. **MOLOTOV COCKTAIL** 66
32. **MATTRESS** 67
33. **1:42 AM (A Very Separate Occasion)** 68
34. **THAT YOU EXIST** 69

***All poems written between 10:00 PM and 4 AM with minimum revision/editing

Well we won't begin by over thinking the matter
Or end with editing the results

...So...

I guess
This is as good a place to start as any?

DARLING BY STARLIGHT

There can be no sure telling
My love
Alas
I am not that good
And what follows

This thing...

Won't be for everyone.

I pulled and set myself apart
For you

So I am not full match for anyone else
And this

Well...
I am not sure of it

It has holes
You didn't fill
Questions I could fall through
A great distance
And die atop
Gaps of logic
Closed only by the leaps of faith
That it is bringing me somehow closer to you then not

It's an uncapped circle
Looping into self
And out
Searching for somewhere
Like that sunrise called soon again
Where we will be the noon
We thought we were headed to

Where we will auburn
As the skies we love under

If until that time
Hope is allowed

I am for it
And not free from it
If you can remember that just because
It's Late
Doesn't mean it's dark.
Then that will be enough trust
For me
To Love
Whatever light
Leads in your direction
Darling.

1:27 AM (TILL...)

She could never kiss me
The way you say
You never will

He will never hold you
The way I always would
And there can be no happy endings without
Complicated truth

We are complicated
Are we not?

I can continue to call us progress
Or you can continue to call us off
And it will not matter
Love such as ours
Resists structure as master
Balances itself on myth
Grows apart from us
With disaster

Our ideas
Are just a pathetic best pitch
On where we would head us
Or pause us

Our stop
Sign
All
Read
This
To
Nowhere

We have no control.
We are the soul of this matter
It runs us now.

Tell me to stop
I dare you

And
I will still chase you like the starving thing
I am

I will still adore you like I am dying
Cause we are

I will still love you,
Like you love me back
Cause you do

And

Heart/Melody/ Darling

If I own only the truth in your denial
If I am the lonely only of us unashamed
I will hold us up naked to the world
Unworthy and incapable of understanding
We are the inappropriate
Worth defending
Worth reading
Worth believing in
Till there are no more ends of the earth
To hide lovers and/or faith

Whose kisses swallow poems
Whose lingering hugs
Are strong holds
Refusing to let them go
Or give them up.

GENESIS (First Light)

And so it is...

He stood there waiting
For the debating dawn to spring herself forth as a living tongue
Singing truth atop his young dark nothing
Of which we are told
Nothing wondrous or worthy could come from
A lie Pre-galaxy packaged and sold

With truth
In her
Being
Opposing Omni-presence
Necessary to all things constructive

She amply builds in him
With brilliance
Splitting the matter
Into half light
Hope
Molding his dark with a fantastic ray
Of blind all purpose faith
With questionable promise
Of fulfillment

But hope has power

When the shaded cosmic opposites
Set a course of kiss towards kiss
They diametrically explode
And make planets by promise
And moons when parting
But the sun when they come to the edge
Of again
And again
And again
And again

So lady light
Sing your truth in revolution atop this young dark nothing

And I will defend your decision to have me
By spinning joyous
Proof of abundance.
See what I could be
If you whisper madly to my youth?

Bend me to your will
Conqueror me in creation
And fill the word of me with useful life
Give my void ecstasy
Give my void intimacy
Lend to my limit
Infinite as day to night
And there I promise you will find the joy of your purpose

Because givers are always present at first light…
Givers are always present at first light…
Givers are always present at first light…

11:13 P.M

I can't stop thinking of her
I am not proud of these thoughts
They take me fever forward
Into every deep place
I should never be allowed
My hand on her Rome
My mouth on her London
My tongue in her Paris
My head in her cloud

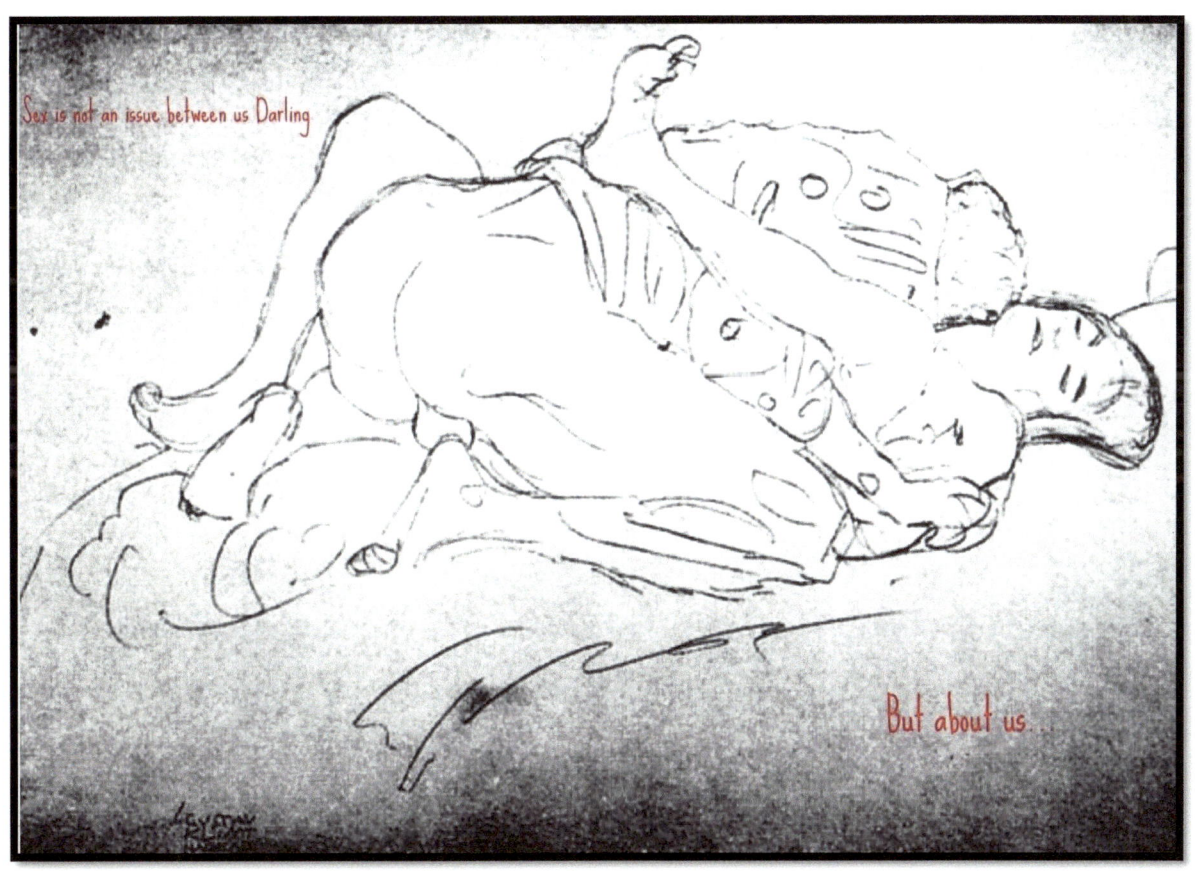

WHAT ESCAPES ME

I admit
You are more what I make of you then anything else

Abstraction obstructed by the ether of myth
Helped along by my heavy sense of heartfelt ethos
Failing
Falling apart from itself
By risk
On the way down
Flailing arms wishing they were wings
Down
Down
All the way down to the truth

A back pack filled with gold
Is useless
When what I need is a parachute

You are the nothing worth all this
Bottom smashed hardness

What you are
Betrays the idea of what you should have been
Betrays the ideal of maybe it could be best for me if
You never existed
I'd never then have had something upon which to dote
To obsess
To criticize
To hope for
To dismiss
And to be dismissed by
To treasure
To harass
To chase
Want
Wish
To wander towards
To have a while
To lose
To get back
And never keep

Because this tricky vice grip
Is hanging me higher then I want to hold on for

Admitting now

That daylight breaks my heart if dawn does not accompany your silhouette
And night is all I wish for if it is accompanied by your whisper
And you curse me down to my bones
And through my gift
To wit I write endless
Obnoxious poems
Which I am sick to the core of
Beaten and broken down in rewind
Don't want any more of
But better this
I think
Prosaic
Violence
Fluff and Nonsense
Poems paltry and indulgent
Then never having loved at all

I admit

For a while now I have known

You are more what I make of you then anything else
And probably the most impressively useless thing I have built
That I don't own

PLEASURE DELAYER

I love the idea of my exposed flesh
Suffering a pinched desire to the point nerves experience napalm death
Exploding me up and from my precipice
I will tell you how good
Her GREAT gets
When I get there

If it all adds up to penetration with substance
And/or masturbation with company
Then all is well that begins
Only with quality endings
For mine if that requires me being stiff
And unrequited for a certain amount of time
Then I will spite myself for the middle
And be just about fine
When I arrive to it

Mansions do not arise into thin air like miracles
Everything tangible and against nature is first designed
Efforted into existence
Climaxes at their pinnacle
I propose are no different

She is after all my sin filled twin tower
And what goes up would not be as dazzling a creation
Without a brilliant collapse
A sensation worthy of a following
Falling action

She will meet us at the crash site in the end
The pit of our stomachs where as victims our ashen covered butterflies
Will wonder themselves into
Forced feelings
Ad nauseam

Who could survive this?

The moment will echo on the tips of our everywhere
Tingle at the edge of all everything
It will last as long as the feeling before the feeling
And when it is done and properly gone

The songs will cease
The poem will having stretched itself at the margins of breath
Found in a manner
The proper death

Through trembling of wanting
Through the sorrow of aching
And the soreness of hoping
And the breaking each other down
Into the needing for perfectly timely love making
It will expire
And in its place
The reality of a new dawn happy
End
Whenever and
Wherever we choose it

It is daylight
So it is different
I guess I'll wake her ass up
Now
And do it again

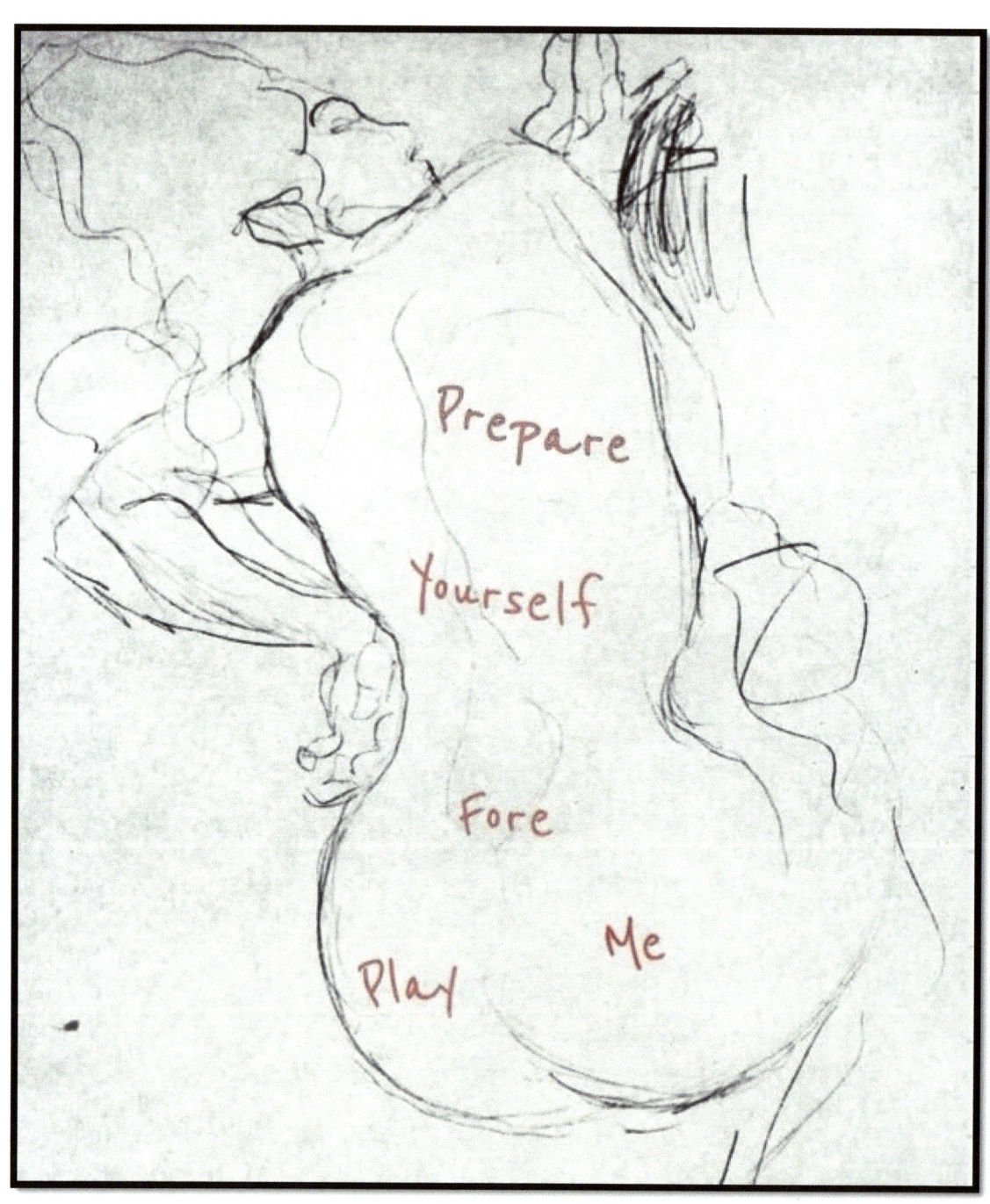

10 PM (ABOUT KISSING)

He wants to jump start life in a kiss
Planted awkwardly
On that foreign half smile
Always tempted he is by those damn exotic full lips

He wants for the high school aggressive first time French
Where nothing is right
But everything is perfect
He wants to suction lock
With fluttering eyes fixing themselves behind lower lidded shade
And hands there fumble dance
Not knowing where to put themselves
Hopping along in their way hopes path
Past all restrictions

He wants tongues to fence fight friendly
And retreat when it gets too much
He wants the breathing to be so heavy
In the rough of it
She mixes signals…
Her "back off" hiss
Moaning itself
Into a steady
Pulling of him to a "come here" place

He wants an endless supply of sudden, lovely, supple,
"ok enough" pecks
Which go on and on
And flight back and forth
To where it started
Working a way to shoulders and fingers
And elbows
And all awkward places

In between

He doesn't know how he wants it to begin
Or where he expects it should end
He just wants
Because he knows
She is wishing his dreams good luck

With every too close smile
And purposefully accidental touch
She is reaching for him to reach back
Because she too wants
-NO HERE IT IS-
She needs to be kissed
Just like that

WHERE IT CAME TO REST

In the rough seat of my pocket
Beats a secret
Hid just an inch or two within plain sight.
Cowardice keeps it tucked away
Complaining of rain
Delaying chance
Questioning the flight back
To the right side
Of where it belongs
Semi conscious of poor choices and bleeding
Racked with pain from self indulgent displacement
It would rather suffer death and judgment
Then rest side by shoulder
Next to the memories of HER that never happen

It would rather clench fire to heaven
Then open fist to fingers
Tracing the heaviness of a stone silhouette

It may never see the world again

It knows too much
Regrets too little
And is so easily upset
That it is now sensitive to any touch but my own

Devoid of purpose
Adverse to risk
It sits sacked in idle
Behind my back
Below my waist
It has come to rest
In a most awkward
But fitting place

As it would rather die in the dark of my pocket
Then live in the black of my chest

"YES" to Empress Submission

Yes!

These chains are a perfect fit
They after all have your last name on them
And have numbed the place you tore and ripped

Shackles have wore their way into me
To the point I now submit
To wearing your abuses as second skin

Yes!

This bull is now yours by prodding
And here he remains chained at the neck
All the same nodding yes!
To the idea of you
Stooping to my level just to dismiss me as another prisoner

Yes!

There are two ways to taste spit
But when you are desirous
You're hard up to take either as disrespect

Yes!

I like that you don't look to me the same way twice
So sometimes in your eye contact
There is a gentle touch
And other times it is serrated
Has edges to cut the guts out of me
Spills all these butterflies I been holding

I like that with intimacy you rattle my cage
And leave
As if it were a test to spur me on
Your heels creating creases in the pavement
That if I were free to believe in progress

May just lead me to you
Or my death

But I am fine staying caged here
Just to praise your design
And secretly
I fear I may break this
If I push too hard on from the inside
If I mess with your pride
Second guess your strength
I will lose the best bit of pain that reminds me I am alive
To fret how it is never enough
Touching or tasting or sampling
The not yet
The maybe later
Those soft kisses
The perfect amount of wetness on your lips
I drown in your words
And marvel at your absurd ability to keep me captive
And even if free I won't give chase
Cause here I am much less a victim
Then I am safe
Here I only imagine you
Here I only wait
And you come back for a bit
And I taste
And then you're off again
Plate in hand
Here there is enough distance
That "yes" is just a one word echo
That I scream into infinity
Only to be certain of its return
Never leaving me lonely
Never making a mess
By mating itself with "no" until
Negatives and positive charges
Gives stillbirth to words lacking breath to sustain them

I don't desire freedom's prison
For my love to chase someone who is walking away
That will never love
THIS Love back.

So I will stay if you don't mind
Caged till you find me

Yes!

Same place
Same time
Empress

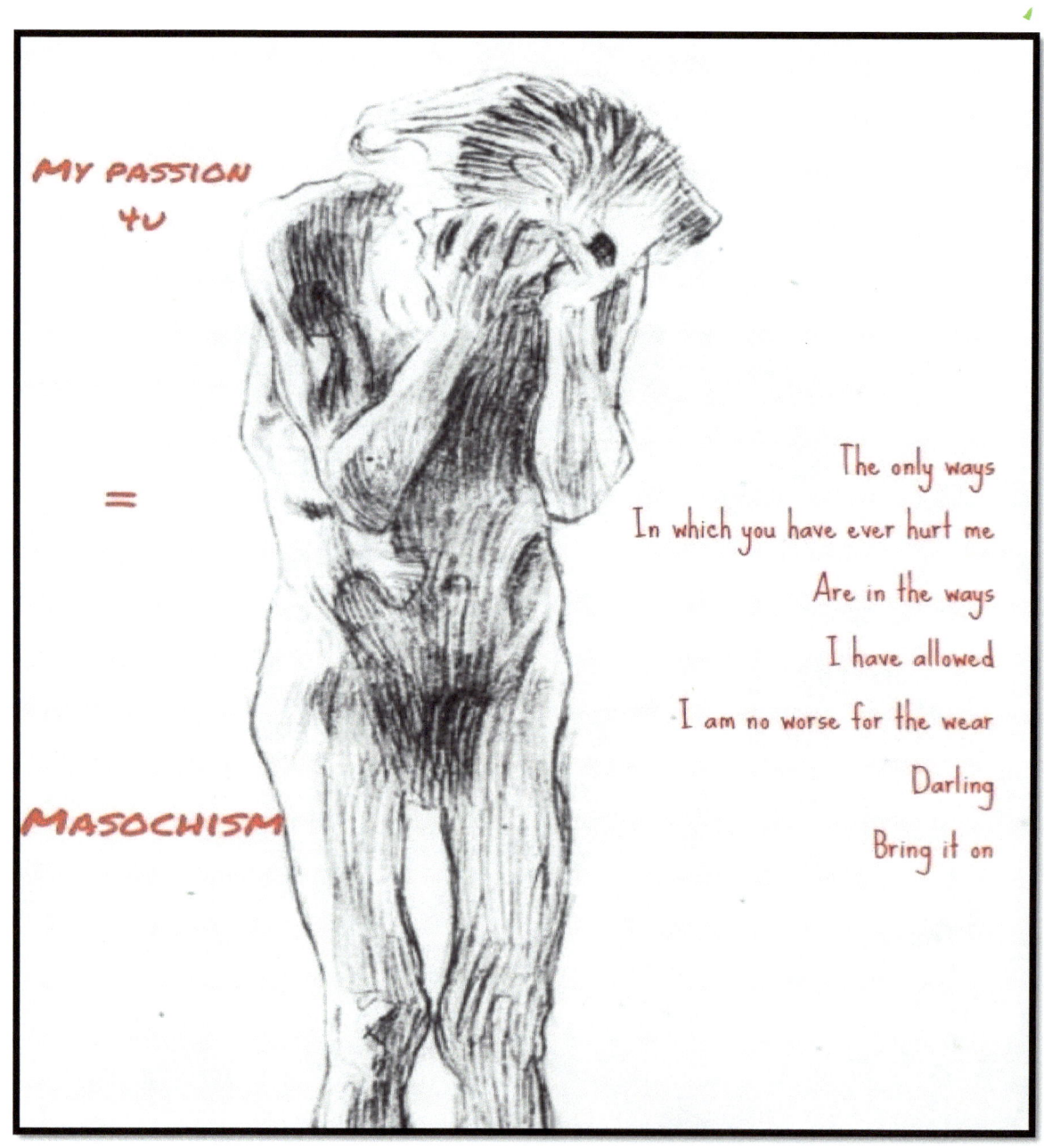

WHERE THE FOX WILL HIDE

There is this garden I know of
With a gold plated gate
And silver locks
A rustic chic

Amidst its middle required for entry
An old fashioned turn-key
And that is the only thing keeping everybody out

Everybody but me.

At this gate others surround and are sated
The gaudy beauty of it
Is where their true interests stop
But I have climbed an unsteady oak tree
Perched atop its branches
And from its impossible angles have seen the true bounty

A miracle garden
I have watched grow cold
Where in even summers possessive heat
Winter weeps snow
And on this abashed Eden
No one dare ask for
And no one cares to sew
There have I set
My choicest love

Soon enough

It will find me

But I will not wait
At the common gate as others…
And will not break anything in the entry
I am more than a clever fox
And will make finding the key for the life of the land my responsibility
As I am also the intended Gardner of this unclaimed lot

Just before the wonder thaws
And makes it something green and ordinary

I will breach its best defense
Will press the flesh of my naked paw
Into the brisk of its endless winter
Whisper to its supposed flaws

That not for a modest fall
Or a temperate spring
Do I ever wish it to risk its divinity
In the shade of another season again

My cold Garden
I love you
Don't ever change a thing

BLOODLUST GOODBYE

My warrior woman
My blood lust
My must have
My never maybe
My everything
My unending want
The Persephone
To My Hades

The pen that weeps Shakespeare
Bleeds you
My dark lady

Dear unquenchable fire
Dear questionable sonnet
Dear unyielding desire
Dear beautiful
Mesmerizing
Unconscionable liar

How your forked tongue
Speaks your own perfections
And yet I remain inspired

And yet I remain weak
And yet I remain of the two of us
The responsible party to reap
Whatever we have BOTH sewn in the deep

And yet I will sleep in your contempt
And wake up in your shame
And live in poems
You've tented me in
Rent free
This is not a home
This is not a destiny
This is not my blame
This is what it sounds like
To lose all of me
In obsession
As penalty

Of loving touch and not letting go
You inside me
I inside you
As these things grow
Who is the tumor
And whose is whose
And who the hell knows?

And who the hells cares

Probably us both
What a pair we make
Your pity
And my woe
The only thing we have properly shared
The only tenant of our faith
Less obvious then our fear
That we can't live for the future
Cause we can't make it here

And as it overflows
So it ends
And so we overthrow this and let it die
Without a goodbye or a whimper
Semper fi
We mutually kiss away the possibility of tears
Through dry and certain eyes
We spy a future
Without each other

Too many scenarios
Too little
Too late
Too many reasons to offer up
One more uproarious lie
To the quiet truth
We have no further use
For
"why"

2:20 AM (Me On The Menu)

Tonight I won't write your poem
I'll bite spitefully at your memory
Spit out the loud bits of spirit
In napkin of silence
Wipe and toss off
As if you were a trash bin nothing
The bitter will cost me a much better poem
Then this

I'll risk
Losing it all
With your blood in my mouth
Your skin in my spit
Our bond between my teeth
I will chew
I will dismantle
I will be petty
I will eschew the subject of us
I assure you I will swallow, hard and deep
And let the meat of the matter
Topple awkwardly down into belly
Of self defeatist deceit

The conceit you must admit
Is as stupid
As it is inspired
Fighting this feeling
Into feeling this fight
Is all tough dinner for naught
Love delicious
Or hate disgusting
The poet is in the end
Caught
Between
Being the meal

And the chef
A self serving victim
All food for thought

TO THE LAMB NAMED HER
(4:00 AM)

Bleed out!
I want your red above my door
Spell my name
Impossible
With a new born hiragana
Something symbolically suffusing love and suffering
Ink your entire self
In treason noted above
And below
Bend at the waist
To the ankles
Bed me
And in so doing
Aid and abet me
Against the rigid law of the Gods
And the exactness of their Angels
Dear Lamb
Be my loophole
My defense strategy
The only thing between my death
And my reason
Be the impure Passover
And in the AM season
I will cleanse my palette of all despair
And lick your despicable clean
I will have found a life outside all Old Testament meanings
And oddly come to understand mercy
The long way
Your body could be the greatest bit of humanity
Left for me to live on
And live on I will
Just spill for me all out
Till your all in,

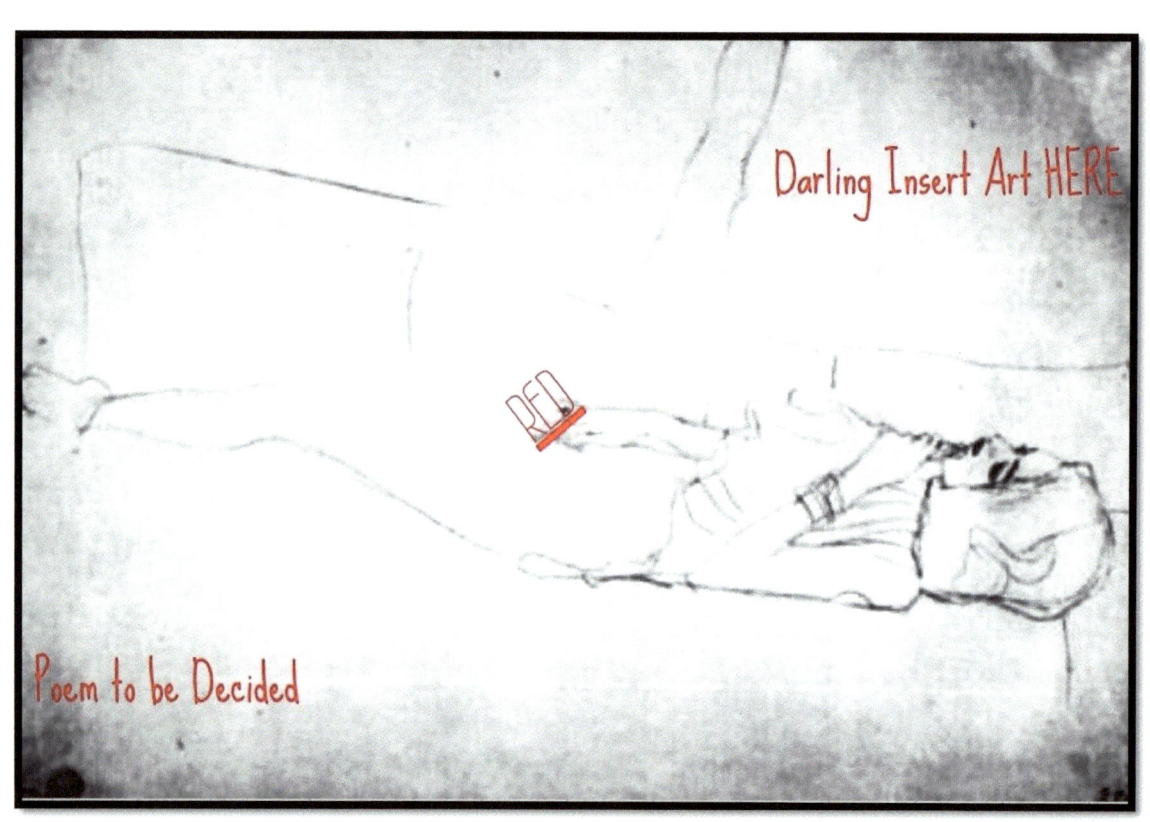

11:58 PM

Want to whisper your name in private
Make love to you in public
Sorry
These nights I often confuse
The what
The where
And when
All that exactness remains lost
In ever changing abstraction
But the who remains sacred
As you
With my heart
And ownership of best sins
A secret
Not so secret
My scarlet letter
Now opened

An open letter
Penned public and poetic to a distant love
And ever darling friend
Who I write all things for

A shameless degree off from understanding
What it takes to truly have you under me
And what's more
Me over you.

I want to leave you in the now
And make love to you then
And curse you the day before that
So the make up can be perfection

I want to say it all wrong
Do it all wrong
And do that all again
Till mixed signals
Joint depression
Mutual inspiration
And wonton NEED
Has us arriving at an even ending neither promised.
Neither understood
And both forgot how to question

GIVE ME YOUR SIN
(To Sound like Something Scrawled on a Subway Bathroom Wall)

Give me the sin of you
Cause the thought is much more of an abstract abomination

Give me your most mortal end
I don't like wallowing in the desperate gutter of imagination

So...

Give me the sin

The one that as your "friend"
I know you are going to do again anyway

Fair truth
It is my turn
So really I'd love a shot at being what is next on your regret list
I earned your fire
Your fury
Your reckless passion
Burned under our every false scripture
In each text message.

My dragon lady
I see
Clearly you are going to do it anyway

Why not make your "anyway" me?

The one who loosed you free
Just to chain you back
In mental chess

So I have you thinking this is friend zone
Why?
Cause we are friendly?

Thought I threw my favorite fish back in the sea?
When in fact I only relaxed the twine
That as you are eternally mine
Grips you closer to me

And it only takes throwing just a short line or two
For you to find your home back on my boat
And at a loss for air
In a hell of whatever
I define you to be

Hellion
Give me Rome
Give me Sodom and Gomorrah
In your instinct is hypocrisy
I want to own land in the twin cities of your rebellion
Before forgiveness
Humility
And holiness finds you cleansed

Give me your sin
Before the closing

Give me not your hand
I have no interest in playground
Pretend marriages

Give me for the sake of all that I understand
Oh how you like being taken in the advantage
And played
And laid low
So that in 3 days times
You can raise him in yourself defined forgiveness
Of your intentionally internally twisted sorrows

I want to be that sword that saws you
I have died to your innocence
And would rather
Now kill by your decadent word

Give me your sin!

I understand how your body bends
What lies your forked tongue has licked
What things you have done once
And swore you'd never again

Until you did them again

Cause of course follies are always better
The next time you tell yourself
You will not depend on them

Always better trying to catch that first time

And you feed on regret
Which makes heavier
The pleasure of caving
So let me be your worst time

Give me your sin!
Give me ALL your sin!!

Give me those things you swore to keep
Even secret from your husband
Give me passion instead of title
Pleasure instead of position
Lies over honesty
And moments over future promise...

We need debauchery to come between us

Let's enter heaven backwards
Likes rogue Shiites and Sunnis
And explode upward till we are nothing more than a casualty
Sprung forth from a casual lie
That anything this powerful
Could ever die gradually

Face to face
Scandal on scandal
Skin on skin
Let us mask the shade of our disgrace
And the age of our joint depression
In scented candles
And for once burn worth something
Not calling each other back in the morning

I will love you only the way you deem appropriate
I will love you anonymously
Erotically

Let us risk nothing
Lose all
And never again

For you are more sin
Then anything else

Give me your indecent self
And in return

I will never return you
To the previous owner's possession

Give me your sin!

Darling...if I wound
Let your scars serve as proof
You have always been the better beast

Darling

Can I make it up to you with a dream?

Well

that's what I am selling

so....

KISS AT THE RIGHT TIME

Want to kiss you there
In the not so mystical place
Between infinity and everywhere
Kiss you like
It is just not right at Park Place or the Boardwalk
Or anywhere else

Kiss you like
I need you right here
In between honking horns and sirens
And silent disapproving stares of the passers by
They don't share this star gaze
And are destined to wander an unslowed lifetime wondering why
For us this is precious
For us this is dear
For us this is one moment saccharine sexy
And crystalline clear
They will never understand
If they were born here.
Why for us the blood thickens
And passion grows
And caution succumbs to desire
And action overthrows tact and fear
Because there is no place made more perfect
Then this not so mystical space
Between infinity and everywhere
A place made complex
By Geeks, Gods and Architects
To share something as simple as this
As precious as kiss...
...me there
...in Time Square

2:43 AM

Somewhere into 2AM and the imagination
Has now made the sin between us finite
You for the win
And I

Move onto hiding it in lascivious poems
Licking these wounds
Calling it depression as progress
My mistake
Was to all in everything
Only to be staked
Permanently on the losing end
Cards shown
Chances blown
Playing for and at once against you
This perpetually weak hand
Till we arrive at my sunrise champion
Surprise!
It's you again
And again
And again

If the devil is a liar
And the Goddess is his devil
Then what are we to make
Of the fiction between them?
What is pleasure for the taking
What is taking at her never
What is a little one sided want between friends?
All unclear
And unfair as now
The feeling worth the weight
Of his pained body
Just a pathetic and wonton orgasm
Thrust into nowhere
His words reduced to her

Nothing
Momentum
Bows
Descends
Falls
Into her downward spiral
His Desires
At 2AM

SOUTH HEAVEN / NORTH EDEN

Wish your nails
Were talons sharp as switch blades
To chase a design of crimson
Vertical across my veins
Splaying me open
Leaving a blood stained mark of misery
Wherever we first lay
So that if we dare it
I die that day

Wish your lips were glossed in aged absinthe
Dipped in a coat of Nightshade
Your tongue dripping Japanese Ivy
Your teeth polished fangs
So that death by kiss
Was certainly hanging in the balance
The closer we came to it
That cosmic justice
Would make the impact as painful
As it was passionate
Violent as it was intentional

Simply put
I want to die by you
So kindly cancel me
Cut me at the knees
Saw me at the sinews
So I can no longer stand
Pull the trigger again and again
Empty the rounds in me
Because love is war
And I believe you would make a much better enemy
Then you ever would friend
And misnaming us allies?
Would be more complicated and painful
So why don't you have compassion and do it

So I don't have to die by my own hand

Push me from the clouds
Let me fall

Into a displaced Heaven
North of regret
South of Eden

Abandon me in that dark
Break me at that bend
End me entirely
Do all this
But most importantly
Never love me
Appropriately
Again

3:46 AM (Planet me)

I can't abide this feeling
My body a habitually lonely
Numb unnecessary thing
An Uninhabited planet
With fair real estate to stretch as far as desires length
And space to tuck itself in comfort under all the furthest stars

But no oxygen

Terrain all mountainous
Dangerous
Detached
Foreign

It peaks Unconquered
Limbs not speaking to one another
Untouched

The sun's company a few months
And many quiet moons away

I would not choose to exist under this cloudless heaven alone

I'd rather be an auburn town
On a dying rock
Lit aflame
With violence,
Noise,
Pollution
And all the choking capital city chaos of life.

Then Eden
Sacred,
Simple
And secreted to silence.

If I am to be truly happy
I will require visitors.

So please

Plague my crops
Oil my ocean
Torch my sky

Just stop to see me sometime.

DEATH AS PROGRESS... A LOVE POEM

She tells me lately she fears what she shares with me
And that somewhere in being unreasonable
We should learn to take what we dare easy
But I am not present inside myself
I am lost in her nowhere
Night through noon.
And I can't shake her
No way
No how
I swoon
I desire her death
I swan dive to my doom
I covet
I convert
I confess
Only waist deep inside her womb do I ever find peace
To misplace
And pressure grip
And pleasure choke till it is blue in the face
And white in the lips

I ask
I seek
I receive
And obsess
Grasp
Squeeze
Tighten the hold on whatever we call this
Vice
Till it has taken life
And left it slip limp in my clutch

This to know that my touch still has power
This to be even handed or rough
This to sentence or pardon
This to trust and let go only after I have said so
Love can be death
And death can be progress
I promise
Whether we know it or not.

LAZY HORNS

Maybe
You and me can drag along our lazy horns
Piped through Davis' mouth
A touch of blue at dawn
Stretched out a bar too long
The sweetest mistake
The most righteous version of wrong

I didn't need you to save my beat
Change my song
Play with me this way
I just wanted to see the curve of your hymn
Complimented by the breakdown of day
After the complex of night
Fall...
Breathe sister breathe
And I will do the same
This is a commitment
As sacred as sharing rings
Or last names
Understanding chemistry
How to change tempo and direction
How to display passion, fury, affection
Just to love this for the moment

Loveless and lost previously
Through this solitary session
We took this fraction of an hour
The pulse of this minute
The wonder of this second
To instill perfection
To create an instant classic
To share a lesson
On the glory of improvisation....

Just breathe with me...
Air to my lungs
And play till young light
Sweeps the night to dawn
Break this down for me
With me

Through me
2 Horns
Over a rhythm
Confident,
Unfettered,
Crazy
Overreaching,
Unending and
Yes lazy
To love any other way

DOUBLE NEGATIVE

I am better without you

That cold open
Was not a mistake

That is in fact, a reality I could check,
And state honestly
While falling from a mountain peak,
Naked, starving and on fire.
Just to escape...
You
Plague upon my first sight
Tragedy played upon my best desires
And all the well wishing you away
And out
Will not work

See just because I love you
Doesn't mean I haven't come to doubt our outcome
Doesn't mean that this all can't be pulled inside out to hurt

Two souls rejected intuition
Flirting dirty
Till transition
Found us atop our hour
Positioning ripe sin into full penetrated fruition
The penalty of which is how quickly fruit sours
The inertia of it all
Is still on my tongue
Rushing down
Into my pit
And my pen
Rises the bitter
Poems
Till I am spitting you back up again
And the taste
Tells me you are worst
Just dessert possible
Just because YOU find me perfect
Doesn't mean that perfection isn't my biggest mistake

Just because I love you
Doesn't mean

I don't also have really bad taste.

I WILL LET HIM LIVE

In the old days
It would have ended with honor
Over my dead body
Or his

A sword causing one to fall on his shield
A punctured lung or rib
A nasty too deep gash
Ends the argument at last
The one that lives
Is the one that loves on
And the other is martyred
Mourned
And in her memory only
Doted upon

We would bury him properly
Before we stepped him over
Shoved him in a shallow grave
For shallower reasons
I would post only
Public pride in this treason
Take his children, title, land
And your most fair hand
From his coldness
And once he lay still
I,
For what it's worth
Would have won the right to be guiltless

Because I would have had to come straight
Yelled his name at your morning gate
And staked my claim
With the stopping of his heart
Aimed at the very private beating of yours
And following this
Most sacrilegious
And intimate of Holy Wars
We would be at peace

But not today...

Today I am more assassin
Then warrior
More foul then beast
And for your attentions and affections
I have to be the least of my strength
Least he find a thief amidst his shadow

He outranks me
So I outflank him
If he is a tank
I am an RPG fired from a friendly
He never realizes I am an enemy
And never saw me coming
Enmity to his home
The mistake he could not have known better to make
And so the texts keep going
Over his head
And the emails fiber optically under his nose
Hide nothing
Cause he is not aware
Not even in the know
That I am inside his love everywhere

It's just the impurity of the thing
The fascination of sharing his thrill
So very clever am I
Messing with her high hopes
And aspirations
Creating a prescription of love
That only I can fulfill
I
BANG! BANG!
Aim
To feel something fantastically fake
And in so doing
Kill something underwhelmingly real

Pity
I will not resolve this
I do not owe him that much
But in the touching
And corrupting his woman
I feel what is being lost

In fairness
Disrupting moral balance
By sneaking
And in our inboxes harmful and inevitable
As missiles are heat seeking
And when it blows up perfect
I ask her only to pretend
This won't end badly
This is not happening by her hand
I teach her to look the other way
As I do him in

As blood splatters coats over households slain
In the now mid due process
Of changing her area code
And last name
And when it falls down
I promise I will leave him living
Maimed a little
Tamed a little
Without love
And without ever being a whole man
Quite the same
And this treachery
Wickedness
This indirect conflict between men
For a woman
Is a damn shame

OUR THERE?

The speed of it was such a
Last and terrible thing
The drop an artful unfair wonder
Are we done now?
Was is it old then?
Where did we come apart from
What did we learn from forced adaptation?
If our there
Is nothing more than the isolation
We tried to avoid
Drawing us further in
By spinning us deeper away
Then we've ever been
Tossing us off alone
To distant and disparate ends

If our there
Is a not exactly fit for two sized island

You were the one who should have known better

Causing me to question

How you could allow me
To fall in love with such thing as you
And dare continue to call me friend?

MOLOCH

I did not build this for me
There is no such thing as free will
Once she is involved
No escaping her
Not in Canaa
Galilee
Not even in Nazareth
Or the Nazarene
This relic of Egypt
Is here on every old testament tongue
Ever present
In every new obscene thought
Anointing now
Belongs to the queen
Damnation is now her 4 walled country

This messiah
Commands dominion over all holy and happy there

I find myself in too much debt to her
Having pledged so much death to her
Buried somewhere are my soldiers in her defense
Beneath gardens in her honor
I have built a house around this destruction
Letting no one in
Weeping ceaselessly in our temple for her presence
And in her absence
Abandon days
For something I believe worth the lack of sleep

At the base of her Pyramid I have fallen deep
In or From?
Love
Having impaled myself somewhere at her peak

And so statuses
And statutes erected
Reflect only a certain malady
The kind wonton and desperate
Of a madman
Wanting miracles
From

A Goddess
Who doesn't speak
To her creator?

Or creature?
Whichever I be
Somewhere between fully realized and exceptionally lonely
Sits a master builder and his company
A sort of well designed
Keep sake
His live body could collapse from exhausting hope
Built at the height of love
And being resigned to see it suffer an ever still born defeat

He is ever the stalwart dedicated to the nothing here
That functions as divinity or salvation
And if you where there
You'd sometimes catch
Him?
Me?
Shrugging to the idea that worship is sweet enough
The monument and temple
Is after all here for witnessing
Or warning
That love is for fools
Or for those who really want to
Believe?
See?
With their own eyes
Just how big a God(dess) can be.

OEDIPUS BY HARP

She plays Oedipus by harp
Strings attached to his veins and valves
Not too far from heart crushed by her playing
And her prying lyre
Alluring as much as
Reigning havoc in his history
Paining him with blood stream sickness
He hears her in everything
And the thickness of sound crashes upon him
Strumming waves of mastery and mystery
Misery and motivation
And he can't have her
Just hear her
She is in the music
The music is in a tome floating away from him
And his sour notes find him alone
Searching solo for the home he thought he found
In all her worldly sounds
Tells a story
With no mention of him
Her love poem with his borrowed instrument
Played as grimly edited fiction
A cruelly hand penned auto-hagiography
Leaving him inkless

And if she had asked

He would gladly go about the thankless task of strangling his own father
To hear her cry
STOP
Burn cities in her name
So that the proper questions could arise
Top bound
Past their surface

So she can see in his violence
The power of his throne at last clearly
And ask
All he ever really wanted to hear

All this for me?

Music to a young king's ears

IN PAST TENSE

I am very lucky to have had you...

Is an easy way in so few words
To betray my original opening line of logic
Degrade, censor and stricture my truth
With a lightly romantic structured sentence
Dispassionately political as it is non-specifically polite

Counter-productive lately
How try as I might to appease my favorite lie upfront
It remains unimpressed
But so hard wired am I
Even
When it hurts
I poetically act in its best defense
While taking real pains to print
Feels impossible
Right now for instance
As I type
I am tapering off the curse words
Tampering with the criticisms
Edging her bitter ends
Cooling my hot cynicism
See not only is it difficult to hide how much I want to be liked
There is an admittedly off chance she might read this
And grab hold of our real insight

But my interest is not just in committing the sin
But purging myself in confession
Till I am heretofore forced to amend this poem in post
Convince my pen to be brutally honest again
Self induced sedition as a brand
Is me demanding more of myself
As I see need in my life for the repetition of hurtful truths
Whereupon performance this poet can takes painful dramatic license

Till artistically it comes to some therapeutic use

She is not here anymore
And will likely be gone a good forever

So all the dutifully kind editing
The kind of editing to this point
Is moot

Sit up straight and write Shariff
Square the shoulders the way proud men do
And finish
With words uncomplicated honest and few
Dear Love, I was very unfortunate to have ever HAD you.

WITH COLOR

Dear unique Bloodlust
Dear Passion Pixie
Dear Fay wonderfully realized
And desirously corrupt

Don't ever be reasonable
Don't let sensible things
Like expectations
Or acceptable haircuts
Career paths
Or wardrobe choices
Dull you
Down
To the numb voice of a
Last nerve

Live loudly
So as to expect
Your contrasting shade
Will be heard
Above the dumb
Dull
Deaf of it all

Be sensational
Leave highlights in
Retain color
As complicated as truth
Dye all the radical you can summon to your damn roots
Find your evidence
Be your proof of it

Don't ever let ordinary in

Don't ever succumb

Keeping in mind
That a reasonable anything
Leads to being an average everyone

3:11 AM...(And Now I am Just Rambling)

Why are you on the inside of everything?
That begins without request
Where did I?
When did I?
Why does the defense rest?
Without fight or care
When the best argument is so worth
Putting my fist in the air
Or at least through something in protest!

The failure balls me right down
Numb
to my future
From the left side of my chest
Caved in long ago
Lacking courage
For danger
It gave in
To some disappointment
Was accosted by some grievous loss
And then there was stress
Always stress

So it opened and accepted
An unfair
Unbalanced
Ungrateful love
Allowed to fester
And cancer into some symbiotic progress
To make it work
It plays on me always
Hard,

And loose with the relationships facts
Inside
I have
So little of me left
Dying
That I need to find the better half here
With you

My one last best chance
To find some use for the rest of my wandering hope
If hope alone

Is worth the living
Tell me again
Tell me again
My love
Why are you on the inside of everything?

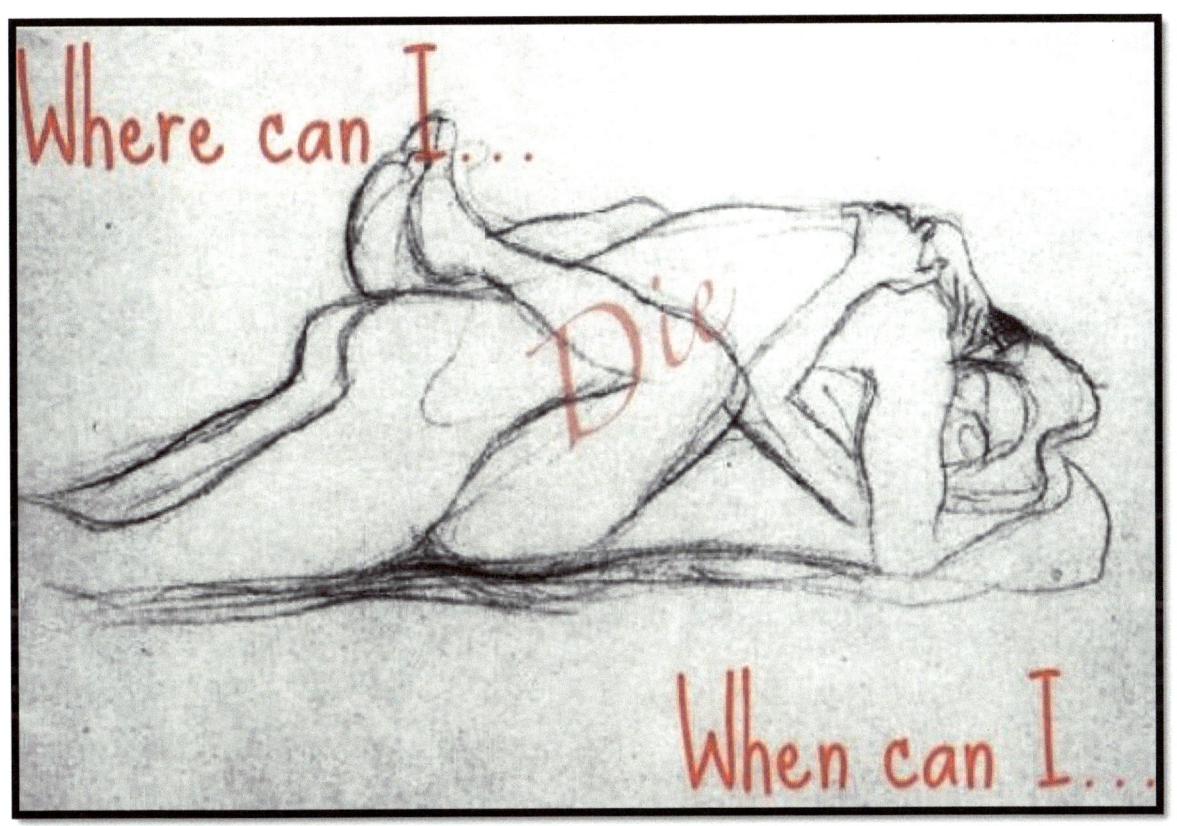

MOLOTOV COCKTAIL

I am certain
Someone threw it for my end
But it landed safely in my lap
With no lifetime to wait
My reflexes failed to react
And in fixation
Stayed themselves confused
A muscle death relaxation
Watching dazzle
Hold fizzle
Till
It
EXPLODES!
Me to collapse
It was something amazing
Something to see
Something nearly worth it
Momentarily

...I guess...

Something brilliant
Something violent

Something I am only certain
If given the chance

I would have never thrown back.

MATTRESS

Bouncing from obsession to obsession
And from thing to vile thing
Taking no one,
Leaving nothing.
On my way.
UP
Nowhere headed
Awesome.
Nauseous
Spiraling down
So Sudden
And
Lost
In living and learning.
Translations the firm way

Wet lust on hallow cushion.
Now finds me
Hurting.
Still soft enough to bounce back and backwards.

Happening now,
Happening now.

But what is always happening now
Is me laying on inaction
Comforted
Weary worried, troubled, stone dazed

Lost on it.
Cause she
Is not here.
To push me...
Down
Further

I want to begin at the painful bottom
To have an excuse to
Scream stop!

My back against this
Mattress
Just doesn't feel right
Without her on top.

1:42 AM (A Very Separate Occasion)

All my kin are falling into ash
Chasing light
Sucking flame
While me
I've never cared for a soft glow summer
Or heat in general
I certainly see no appeal in dying in everyone else's direction
I don't want my end to be on a shoulder
So
I think
I'll dip my wings in the deep of the pool
And if I cannot find strength to fly out again
Truly deserve my death
A little wet could be an interesting way to go

And at least there
I am certain to belong to the miracle of nowhere
Called no one else.

THAT YOU EXIST

That your thighs exist
And the space between them
Contains a missing piece of us
That you get to open and close
At your best ease
Or my good pressure
Is temptation enough

That your thick and righteous lips exist
Only to whisper walk those sweet nothings I hold dear
Into the desolate nowhere
That is your empty space of home
Is frustration enough

That I have a side throne empty
But a side thorn present
That I have Queen but not crown
That I have war with no spoils
That I have all fury
But no sound
Is desolation enough

That we share the same sky
With the divine firmament
Proving God is not just faith
But fact
Is to me torturous evidence
Of an almighty power capable of acting
As our best interest actuary
To muddle our fate
Scuttle our best laid plans
Collapse us apart
And away from parsing this
Soul deep loneliness
The Gods don't answer to
Is enough
For me to risk
Turning my back to the heavens and dismiss
My Demi-child heritage
My Semi-divine blood rights.
Just to face the hell you bring direct
I don't believe I will win our war

I confess
But I am not going down without a fight
And won't be staying there without your kiss

I don't know if you like me anymore
Or love me any less
Because of all this
But that you exist
My darling
That I have been close enough by your side all along
To touch most of your aching edges
That I have spent so much time tending to you in the gap of your wounds
I have not arrived back to myself
That I may not survive the mending
That I showed up too soon in your life to help
That I discovered my love too late defend it properly
That we are now all happy middle strands
No base beginning
No tidy end

That you want to consume me like
An enemy lover sometimes
Then dismiss me as a pitiful friend

That sin never was the issue
But more so how it is to be apportioned
Between us
Is enough

That I don't bend and you do
That I lost the new you to somebody old
That I hold only still the truth
That I miss you everyday
And continually will
Despite it being of little use

That you exist
And with you
All the questions
That fraction you up
Into my truth
Into everything that works together for good
To all Answers
To all evidence
To my proof
I am alive and in love with someone worth loving
And that for any man should be enough

*All Art by Γ. Κλιμπτ

www.ingramcontent.com/pod-product-compliance
Lightning Source LLC
Chambersburg PA
CBHW061357090426
42743CB00002B/48